D1488215

CHRISTMAS PROGRAMS
FOR
CHURCH GROUPS

CHRISTMAS PROGRAMS
FOR
CHURCH GROUPS

by
Marilynn A. Smith

BAKER BOOK HOUSE
Grand Rapids, Michigan

ISBN: 0-8010-7910-1

First printing, July 1968
Second printing, November 1968
Third printing, October 1970
Fourth printing, September 1971
Fifth printing, June 1974
Sixth printing, July 1976

PHOTOLITHOPRINTED BY CUSHING - MALLOY, INC.
ANN ARBOR, MICHIGAN, UNITED STATES OF AMERICA
1976

Foreword

The putting together, directing, and presentation of a Christmas program can be an enjoyable and rewarding task. The principle factors to make it a success are: (1) the selection of material that meets the aim and purpose you have in mind, (2) the selection of material the intended participants can handle, and (3) ample time for preparation on the part of both the committee and the participants. Finally, the success of these first three considerations depends upon an additional factor — (4) Make certain that the message is heard clearly! In larger auditoriums this will require the rearrangement of the P.A. system, or the renting of special P.A. equipment. It certainly means checking and rechecking all parts as many times as necessary to make certain that every person in the audience can hear every word uttered. When the above requirements are met, the program is certain to be spiritually rewarding to both the participants and the audience — and God will be glorified. (5) The alertness of the participants and the attention of the audience can be maintained at a high level by limiting the program to a maximum length of one hour.

This book is intended to furnish material to help in constructing an effective program. The material is of a wide variety, and suitable for various age groups. It can be used as presented or modified to suit your particular group.

The program may be kept simple or made complex. Both types are included in this book. Also numerous selections are presented so that substitutions can readily be made, and so that this book can furnish programs with fresh material for many years to come.

— Marilynn A. Smith

Acknowledgment

This is to acknowledge with appreciation the ready and wide response to our request for material to embody in this book of Christmas programs. We are especially indebted to the Midwest Sunday School Association and the several individuals whose names are appended to the programs. We ask the indulgence of any whose offerings are not properly acknowledged, and kindly request that such be called to our attention so that this may be rectified in future printings.

— Marilynn A. Smith

Contents

1. THE CHRISTMAS MESSAGE IN SCRIPTURE AND SONG

Suggestions. Variations may be made in this program as well as in many others throughout this book. Scripture may be from your favorite version. Choral Reading may be by a Speaking Choir especially trained for this purpose, by one of the Senior classes, or by classes of various age groups. The songs, too, may be assigned to the several classes; some may be by the entire audience. Those representing Mary and Joseph, the Shepherds, and the Wise Men should be appropriately costumed. Songs and hymns may be substituted as desired.

PROCESSIONAL: "O Come, O Come, Immanuel"

WELCOME

CHORAL READING: Isaiah 11:1-5, 10

PRAYER

CHORAL READING: Luke 1:36-46

SONG: "My Soul Doth Magnify the Lord"

CHORAL READING: Matthew 2:5-6

SONG: "O Little Town of Bethlehem"

CHORAL READING: Luke 2:17

SONG: "Away in a Manger" (*During the song place manger on stage, and Mary and Joseph appear and stand by the manger, remain to the end of the song, and then exit.*)

CHORAL READING: Luke 2:8-10 (*Three shepherds appear and exit.*)

SONG: "Silent Night"

SONG: "Hark, the Herald Angels Sing"

CHORAL READING: Matthew 2:7-12

BACKGROUND MUSIC (OR SOLO): "What Child Is This?" (*While three Wise Men appear carrying gifts*)

SONG: "We Three Kings" (*by the boys representing the Wise Men. May be assisted by a specially selected singing group or by a Sunday School Class.*)

SONG: "Joy to the World"

CHORAL READING: Matthew 28:1-10

SONG: "For God So Loved the World"

PRAYER OF THANKSGIVING

2. CHRISTMAS — PROPHECY TO FULFILLMENT

Suggestions. See the suggestions for the preceeding program. In this program a Speaking Choir may be used instead of the Narrator. Be sure the Narrator can be clearly heard. A microphone is desirable.

PRELUDE: Medley of Christmas Hymns

NARRATOR: Micah 5:2

ADULT CHOIR: "Hark! What Mean Those Holy Voices"

(10 *seconds silence*)

ADULT AND JUNIOR CHOIR PROCESSIONAL (singing "O Come, All Ye Faithful")

NARRATOR: Luke 2:4-6

ADULT CHOIR, WITH JUNIOR CHOIR ECHOING: "Silent Night"

NARRATOR: Malachi 4:5-6

PRIMARIES: (*March in from back, singing with the Junior Choir, "Away in a Manger"*)

PRIMARIES: (*When arranged on stage*): "O Little Town of Bethlehem" (*go to seats while organ continues playing*)

NARRATOR: Luke 2:7

ADULT CHOIR: "No Room"

NARRATOR: Luke 2:8-12

QUARTET: "While Shepherds Watched Their Flocks by Night"

NARRATOR: Luke 2:13-14

ADULT AND JUNIOR CHOIRS: "Hark, the Herald Angels Sing"

NARRATOR: John 3:16

ADULT CHOIR: "Have You Any Room for Jesus?"

A CHRISTMAS PRAYER: (*the Pastor, or Superintendent*)

SONG: "Joy to the World"

A CHRISTMAS MEDITATION (*the Pastor, or Superintendent*)

SONG: "Come, Thou Long Expected Jesus" (*all*)
   (*10 seconds silence*)

BENEDICTION

POSTLUDE

3.   A CHRISTMAS EVE SERVICE *(flexibility)*

May be used as a church service, or as a devotional in a group meeting, or for public presentation to an invited audience. It may be adapted in many ways.

PRAYER: Pastor or Leader

CAROL: "O Come, All Ye Faithful" *(by congregation, group, or those presenting the program)*

RESPONSIVE READING: *(by a speaking choir, class, or congregation)*

My soul doth magnify the Lord.

And my spirit hath rejoiced in God my Savior.

For he hath regarded the low estate of his handmaiden; for, behold, from henceforth all generations shall call me blessed.

For he that is mighty hath done to me great things, and holy is his name.

And his mercy is on them that fear him from generation to generation.

He hath showed strength with his arm, he hath scattered the proud in the imagination of their hearts.

He hath put down the mighty from their seats, and exalted them of low degree.

He hath filled the hungry with good things, and the rich he hath sent empty away.

He hath helped his servant Israel, in remembrance of his mercy;

As he spake to our fathers, to Abraham, and to his sons forever.

CHRISTMAS SCRIPTURE: Luke 2:8-14

CAROL: "It Came upon a Midnight Clear"

CHRISTMAS SCRIPTURE: Luke 2:1-7

CAROL: "O Little Town of Bethlehem"

CHRISTMAS SCRIPTURE: Luke 2:15-20

CHRISTMAS ANTHEM: "Go Tell It on the Mountain" (*Senior Choir*) Hark the Herald

PRAYER

CHRISTMAS SOLO: "O Holy Night" Joy to the world

CHRISTMAS MEDITATION: The Pastor

CHRISTMAS ANTHEM: "O Savior Sweet," (*Junior Choir*)

CAROL: "Silent Night, Holy Night" (*Audience*)

CHORAL POSTLUDE: "Christians Awake" (*Junior and Senior Choirs*)

PRAYER OR BENEDICTION

—Adapted from the Christmas Eve Service of the United States Air Force Academy, December 24, 1967

4. A CHRISTMAS PROGRAM

(May be used as a candlelight service)

Prelude: (*Christmas music by organ, organ and piano, organ and violin or cello, or selected instruments*)

I. "Silent Night" (*instruments as above*)

Speaking Choir and Young People's Singing Choir march in singing "Silent Night." (All carry candles if this program is given as a candlelight service. They blow out candles before they are seated.) "Silent Night" is played through once by the instruments before the choirs begin marching in.

II. Meditation by Minister (*5-8 minutes*)

III. Song by Young People's Choir: "All My Heart This Night Rejoices"

Children come up from basement or adjoining room, and stand in line waiting to enter the door leading to the platform while the choir is singing their song (III). Children other than the Choirs will remain "backstage" for two reasons: (1) to make the service more worshipful, and (2) to afford greater seating capacity in the sanctuary. Also, interest and an element of surprise is added to the service by the entrance of the several groups.

As each group in IV, V, and VI finishes its part, it steps to the rear of the platform in preparation for the song (VII) in unison.

Nine kindergarten children present the following Acrostic. Each carries a letter.

IV. An Acrostic, "Christmas," (*By Kindergarten*)

C is for the *Christ-Child,*
   The blessed baby boy.
H is for the *Happiness*
   That we this day enjoy.
R is for the *Royalty*
   Of Christ, the little Child.
I is for His *Innocence*
   So pure He was and mild.

15

S   is for the *Songs* of joy
    The Holy angels sang.
T   is for the *Tidings* glad
    That thro' the midnight rang.
M   is for the *Manger* bed
    Where lay the babe so fair.
A   is for *Adoration*
    Of shepherds gathered there.
S   is for *Salvation*
    That Jesus came to bring.

All: Oh, worship Him at Christmas time,
       The Christ Child who is King.

V. Exercise: "Little Candle Bearers," (*For three boys* or girls, each carrying a lighted candle)

All: We are little candle bearers.
       Each one with a tiny light.
       And we want to follow Jesus.
       May our light be always bright.

First: In our home I want to spread
         A bright and happy light.
         I want to show my love to all
         Every day and every night.

Second: The candle I am holding
          Is just a tiny little light.
          I want to be in word and actions
          A light that always shines real bright.

Third: My little candle is but small
         Yet spreads its light around me.

Just so I want to follow Jesus
And spread His light about me.

All: May the light of Christ our Savior
Show the path that we must go.
May He with his love surround us
And save us from eternal woe.

VI. Exercise: "Our Gifts," (*For five primary children*)

All: What shall we give to Jesus
This happy Christmas day
For all the priceless blessings
Strewn all along the way?
For all His care and favor,
His tenderness and love.
What can we give to Jesus
Our gratitude to prove?

First: I'll give my heart to Jesus
With all the love it holds.
For it is His. His kindness
My heart and life enfolds.

Second: I'll give my feet and ever
Walk where the Savior leads;
I'll bear His word, run errands
Hastening to do kind deeds.

Third: My hands shall be my Master's
To work for Him in joy
No task will be too heavy
If He my hands employ.

Fourth: I'll give my strength to Jesus
His holy will to do.

To stand against temptations
Be brave and strong and true.

Fifth: My faith I'll give to Jesus
Nor doubt His love and care;
He, who is my Redeemer
Will all my trials share.

All: We'll give our lives to Jesus
To Him they shall belong;
We'll give Him loving service,
Give praise and prayer and song.
We'll give our best to Jesus,
Not only for this day,
But all our lives will serve Him
His goodness to repay.

VII. Song: "Away in a Manger" (*By the children who have presented IV, V, and VI*)

(*Children leave platform*)

VIII. Speaking Choir: Psalm 24

IX. Song: "Hark the Herald Angels Sing" (*Young People's Choir*)

X. "The Christmas Story," (*By narrator and primary or intermediate children*)

Narrator: It happened in those days, that the Roman emperor Caesar Augustus, who ruled over most of the world, made a law that all the people in his kingdom should pay a tax to the Roman government. He ordered everyone to go to his native city and to stay there till the tax officers came around to tell each man how much money he must pay. Joseph and Mary had to travel to the little town of Bethlehem near Jerusalem to be taxed. They lived in Nazareth, but Joseph had descended from the family of David; and David had lived in Bethlehem.

Bethlehem was a little town. It was crowded at this time, for many people belonging to the family of David had come to be taxed. By the time Joseph and Mary reached the town, every house was full of visitors. No one had room for them. What were they to do? They surely could not stay in the street! There was only one place where they found a welcome. That was a stable where animals were sheltered. Here Mary and Joseph found a bed of soft sweet hay. That night was a blessed night, and that lowly stable became a holy place. For on that night the Savior of the world was born. God sent His own son into the world to be Mary's baby.

Song: "Once in Royal David's City"

(*Enter Mary and Joseph*)

Narrator: How happy Mary was. Her heart was filled with love and adoration. Mary looked at the baby tenderly and adoringly, for she knew that this tiny child was to be the Savior of the world.

(*Enter three children in white to represent angels*)

Narrator: When God's Son was born on earth, heralds came to announce his coming. They were glorious angels, bright and shining.

(*Enter Shepherds*)

Narrator: On the night when Jesus was born, there were shepherds in the fields near Bethlehem, keeping watch over their flocks by night. Suddenly the glory of the Lord shone round about them. A light from heaven, more glorious than the light of the sun, filled the sky. An angel of the Lord came near them, and they were very much afraid.

(*Enter another child in white*)

Narrator: The angel said, "Be not afraid, for behold, I bring you good tidings of great joy, which shall be to all the people. For unto you is born this day in the city of David a Savior, which is Christ the Lord, And this is the sign unto you. You shall find the babe wrapped in swaddling clothes and lying in a manger."

(*Enter a group of children dressed in white to represent the angel choir*)

Narrator: Suddenly the sky was filled with angels, praising God and saying, "Glory to God in the highest, and on earth peace among men in whom He is well pleased." The glory of God was shining over all the earth as if heaven itself were opened, and the shepherds were gazing into it. They forgot their flocks as they gazed at the dazzling glory and listened to the wonderful words.

Song: "While Shepherds Watched Their Flocks by Night" Night"

(*Exit angels*)

Narrator: After the angels had gone back into heaven, the shepherds said one to another, "Let us now go to Bethlehem to see this strange thing which the Lord has made known to us." As fast as they could, they ran to Bethlehem. There, in a stable, they found Joseph and Mary and the baby lying in a manger. They kneeled down in adoration before him.

And the shepherds returned, glorifying and praising God for all the things that they had heard and seen.

(*Exit shepherds*)

(*Enter Wise Men*)

Narrator: One night a month later while wise men were gazing into the sky, they saw a new star, an unusually bright one. This discovery excited them. As they watched the star, it moved. The wise men were sure that it had been sent to guide them to the place where they would find the great king whose coming was foretold by the star. They followed it till they came to Bethlehem. At the very place where the young child was, the star stood still. The wise men went into the house. There they saw the little child whose star they had followed so far, and they kneeled down and worshipped him. Opening their treasures, they took out the precious gifts which they had brought — gold, and rare perfumes called frankincense and myrrh.

Song: "Story of the Wise Men" (*By the Senior Choir*)

(*Children of the Beginner's Department come onto the platform and join the choirs and the congregation in singing* "Joy to the World")

—Arranged by Helen Holkeboer

5. BETHLEHEM

This program can be adapted for a small or larger Sunday School. (It was originally prepared especially for the Hazen Street Mission Sunday School at Grand Rapids, Michigan.) It makes room for the entire Sunday School and the part for each class was written to accommodate the entire number of pupils in it.

Practically all of the text is a direct quotation from Scripture (with the personal pronouns in some cases changed to their more up-to-date forms). Each part is intended for one class. If the number of pupils is greater or smaller than the sections to each part, some sections may be combined or divided to suit the number of pupils.

Equipment Requirements: The setting can be made as elaborate as desired. It can also be kept very simple. The setting can readily be arranged so the stage resembles a town gate. Overhead from one gate post to the other is an arch bearing the name of Bethlehem.

The Narrator may be dressed as an old man in flowing robes and the sheets of the program may be pasted end to end and made into a scroll which he unrolls as the program progresses, making it unnecessary for him to memorize everything in its entirety.

The various characters can have the traditional costumes as circumstances permit. A little ingenuity can accomplish a great deal with bathrobes, blankets and scarfs.

Cast:

Prologue: Narrator

Part I: Narrator; Naomi; Ruth; Boaz; Kinsman; Witnesses (four or more boys)

Part II: Narrator; Jesse and eight sons; Samuel

Part III: Narrator; eight girls or boys

Part IV: Two girls

Part V: Six girls or boys

Part VI: Ten girls or boys

Part VII: Three boys (representing the Wise Men; twelve speakers)

Prologue

Narrator: Bethlehem is a small town more than four thousand years old. Its name was Ephrath when the Pa-

22

triarch Jacob first came upon it. The name was later changed to Bethlehem, which means "House of Bread," probably because it was in the center of a good farming community and produced plenty of food. A great many things have happened in Bethlehem which are recorded in the Bible. Sitting here in the gate of the town we will ask the people who come by this way what these interesting things are.

Part I

Narrator: It came to pass in the days of the judges that Naomi returned to Bethlehem from the land of Moab with her daughter-in-law Ruth (*Naomi and Ruth enter at left of stage.*)

Naomi: Ruth, my daughter-in-law. Go return to your mother's house. "Jehovah deal kindly with you as you have dealt with the dead, and with me. Behold, your sister-in-law is gone back to her people and to her god; return after your sister-in-law."

Ruth: "Entreat me not to leave you, and to return from following after you; for where you go, I will go, and where you lodge, I will lodge; your people shall be my people, and your God my God; where you die I will die and there will I be buried: Jehovah do so to me and more also, if anything but death part you and me."

Narrator: "So these two went until they came to Bethlehem."

(*Enter Boaz at right of stage*)

Boaz: (*bowing to Narrator*) "Jehovah be with you."

Narrator: Jehovah bless you, Boaz. (*Kinsman enters at right of stage*)

Boaz: "Ho, such a one! turn aside" and sit down here. (*Kinsman does so*)

Boaz: (*motioning to witnesses*) This way men, "Sit down here." (*Four or more witnesses come forward and sit down.*)

Boaz: (*To kinsman*) "Naomi, that is come again out of the country of Moab is about to sell the parcel of land which was our brother Elimelech's; and I thought to disclose it to you, saying, Buy it before them that sit here, and before the elders of my people. If you will redeem it, redeem it: but if you will not redeem it, then tell me, that I may know; for there is none other to redeem it besides you; and I am after you."

Kinsman (*To Boaz*) "I will redeem it."

Boaz: "What day you buy the field of the hand of Naomi, you must buy it also of Ruth the Moabitess, the wife of the dead, to raise up the name of the dead upon his inheritance."

Kinsman: "I cannot redeem it for myself, lest I mar my own inheritance: take my right of redemption. . . . buy it for yourself." As a token I give you my shoe. (*Removes shoe and hands it to Boaz*)

Boaz: (*takes shoe and says to witnesses*) "You are witnesses this day, that I have bought all that was Elimelech's . . . of the hand of Naomi."

Witnesses: (*In unison*) We are witnesses.

Narrator: "And Boaz begat Obed, and Obed begat Jesse, and Jesse begat David." (*All leave the stage*)

Part II

(*Jesse and seven sons line up along left wall while Samuel takes his place at right wall*)

Narrator: "And Jehovah said to Samuel: How long will you mourn for Saul, seeing I have rejected him from being

King over Israel? Fill your horn with oil, and go; I will
send you to Jesse the Bethlehemite; for I have provided
me a king from among his sons. . . . And Samuel did
that which Jehovah spoke, and came to Bethlehem."

(*Jesse and sons go on stage from left and Samuel from
the right meeting at center*)

Jesse: "Do you come peaceably?"

Samuel: "Peaceably. I am come to sacrifice to Jehovah:
sanctify yourselves and come with me to the sacrifice."
Jehovah has also sent me to anoint one of your sons to
be king over Israel.

Jesse: Here is Eliab. (*Jesse presents first son*)

Samuel: Surely he is a son of good countenance and
stature; but Jehovah has not chosen him.

Jesse: Here is Abinadab.

Samuel: Neither has Jehovah chosen him.

Jesse: Here is Chammah.

Samuel: Neither has Jehovah chosen him.

Jesse: Is it one of these? (*Pointing to the others*)

Samuel: No, it is not. "Are here all your children?"

Jesse: "There remains yet the youngest, and behold, he is
keeping the sheep."

Samuel: "Send and fetch him; for we will not sit down till
he come hither."

Jesse: (*To one of the sons*) Fetch David. (*Son goes behind
left screen; after a few moments returns with David.
David has harp and sling shot.*)

Narrator: "And Jehovah said, Arise, anoint him; for this is
he."

(*David kneels and Samuel holds horn over his head*)

Narrator: "And the Spirit of the Jehovah came mightily upon David from that day forward." (*All leave the stage*)

SONG: "O Come, O Come, Immanuel"

Part III

Narrator: From the time of David to the coming of the Christ the voice of many prophets were heard.

(*The prophets represented by eight girls or boys appear on the stage.*)

First: The Patriarch Jacob said in Genesis 49:10, "The scepter shall not depart from Judah, nor a lawgiver from between his feet, until Shiloh [that is Peacemaker] come; and to him shall the gathering of the people be."

Second: Moses said in Deuteronomy 18:15, "Jehovah your God will raise up unto you a prophet from the midst of you, of your brethren, like unto me; to him shall you listen."

Third: David said in Psalm 132:11, "Jehovah hath sworn to David in truth; he will not turn from it: Of the fruit of your body will I set upon your throne."

Fourth: Jeremiah prophesied in Jeremiah 23:5, "Behold, the days come, saith Jehovah, that I will raise up unto David a righteous Branch, and he shall reign as king."

Fifth: Balaam prophesied in Numbers 24:17, "I see him, but not now; I behold him, but not nigh: There shall come forth a star out of Jacob."

SONG: "Star of the East" (*By Intermediates*)

Sixth: Micah prophesied in his book, 5:2, "But thou, Bethlehem Ephratah, though thou be little among the thousands of Judah, yet out of thee shall he come forth unto me that is to be ruler in Israel; whose goings forth have been of old, from everlasting."

Seventh: Isaiah prophesied in his book, 7:14, "Therefore the Lord himself will give you a sign; Behold a virgin shall conceive, and bear a son, and shall call his name Immanuel [that is, God with us]."

Eighth: In Isaiah 9:6, 7 we read "For unto us a child is born, unto us a son is given; and the government shall be upon his shoulder: and his name shall be called Wonderful, Counselor, The mighty God, The everlasting Father, The Prince of Peace. Of the increase of his government and peace there shall be no end, upon the throne of David, and upon his kingdom, to order it, and to establish it with judgment and with justice from henceforth even for ever. The zeal of the Lord of hosts will perform this."

(*Sing the Duet from Handel's oratorio, "The Messiah," or an anthem dealing with a prophetic theme.*)

Part IV

Narrator: We have heard the prophecies which foretold the coming of the Christ. Now we shall hear what the angels said at the time the Christ was born.

(*Two girls appear on stage*)

First: Luke 1:30, "And the angel said unto her, Fear not, Mary: for thou hath found favor with God. And behold, thou shalt conceive and bring forth a son, and shalt call his name Jesus. He shall be great, and shall be called the Son of the Most High: and the Lord God shall give unto him the throne of his father David; and he shall reign over the house of Jacob forever; and of his kingdom there shall be no end. The Holy Ghost shall come upon thee, and the power of the Most High shall overshadow thee; wherefore also that which is to be born shall be called holy, the Son of God."

Second: Matthew 1:20-24, "An angel of the Lord appeared unto him in a dream saying: Joseph thou son of David, fear not to take unto thee Mary thy wife; for that which is conceived in her is of the Holy Ghost. And she shall bring forth a son; and thou shalt call his name Jesus, for it is he that shall save his people from their sins. Now all this is come to pass that it might be fulfilled which was spoken by the Lord through the prophet. And Joseph arose from his sleep, and did as the angel of the Lord commanded him."

Part V

Organ: (*"Silent Night, Holy Night"* *is played softly as six speakers come on the stage. This part may also be given effectively by a Speaking Choir.*)

First: "Now it came to pass in those days, there went out a decree from Caesar Augustus, that all the world should be enrolled."

Second: "And all went to enroll themselves, every one to his own city."

Third: "And Joseph also went up from Galilee, out of the city of Nazareth, into Judea, to the city of David, which is called Bethlehem, because he was of the house and family of David."

Fourth: "To enroll himself with Mary, who was bethrothed to him, being great with child."

Fifth: "And it came to pass, while they were there, the days were fulfilled that she should be delivered."

Sixth: "And she brought forth her first born son; and she wrapped Him in swaddling clothes, and laid him in a manger because there was no room for them in the inn."

SONG: "Away in a Manger" (*by the speakers of the above, or by a select group or class*)

Part VI

(*Ten boys or girls*)

First: "And there were shepherds in the same country abiding in the field, and keeping watch by night over their flock."

Second: "And an angel of the Lord stood by them, and the glory of the Lord shone round about them: and they were sore afraid."

Third: "And the angel said unto them, Be not afraid; for behold, I bring you good tidings of great joy which shall be to all people."

Fourth: "For there is born to you this day in the city of David a Saviour, who is Christ the Lord."

Fifth: "And this is the sign unto you; Ye shall find a babe wrapped in swaddling clothes, and lying in a manger."

Sixth: "And suddenly there was with the angel a multitude of the heavenly host praising God, and saying,"

Seventh: "Glory to God in the highest, and on earth peace among men in whom he is well pleased."

Eighth: "And it came to pass, when the angels went away from them into heaven the shepherds said one to another, Let us go now even unto Bethlehem, and see this thing that is come to pass, which the Lord hath made known unto us."

Ninth: "And they came with haste, and found both Mary and Joseph, and the babe lying in the manger."

Tenth: "And when they saw it, they made known concerning the saying which was told them by the angels."

SONG: "It Came upon the Midnight Clear"

Part VII

SONG: "We Three Kings of Orient Are," (*May be sung by three boys in costume*)

(*During the singing of this song, the twelve speakers go on the stage.*)

First: "Lo, the star which they saw in the East went before them, till it came and stood over where the young child was."

Second: "When they saw the star, they rejoiced with exceeding great joy."

Third:
The star that led to Jesus,
In days of long ago,
No longer shines from heaven,
With bright and blessed glow.
But trustful lives, and loving
A fairer radiance show.

Fourth: With words and deeds of kindness,
Star children we would be;
That pilgrims through the darkness
A cheery spark may see,
And turn their weary footsteps
To paths of purity.

Fifth: "And when they were come into the house, they saw the young child with Mary his mother, and fell down, and worshipped Him; and when they had opened their treasures, they presented unto Him gifts; gold, and frankincense, and myrrh."

Sixth: Whoever bears the needy,
 Blest offerings in His name,
 With love's rich gold and incense,
 The Master will proclaim,
 Till all the world be gladdened,
 Because the Christ child came.

Seventh: So shall the many star-beams
 Reflect the one great light,
 Till pride and greed shall vanish,
 Like shadows in the night.
 Till shines high the Dayspring,
 All gloriously bright.

Eight: "Arise, shine; for thy light is come, and the glory of the Lord is risen upon thee."

Ninth: I am peace; my mellow rays,
 Shine to cheer the troubled ways.

Tenth: Good-will am I; of whom the angels say,
 Bear joy to all, upon this Christmas Day.

Eleventh: I am Contentment; why sigh and repine,
 When numberless blessings already are mine?

Twelfth: I am little Cheerfulness.
 I will smile and sing
 Helping others keep with joy
 The birthday of our King.

All: We are all star-children, followers of the King.
 Gladly serving others, while the joy-bells ring;

If, to do His bidding, faithfully we try,
We can add new jewels to the Christmas sky.

SONG: "Jesus Loves the Little Children"

SONG: "Joy to the World" (*by entire Sunday School audience*)

6. JESUS OUR SAVIOR

Suggestions. In all these programs units may be omitted or sub-stituted from other programs to suit the occasion or age group.

The hymns are suggestions and fit the theme of this program. Other hymns may be substituted.

1. HYMN: "Silent Night, Holy Night"

2. WELCOME

(*For three little children carrying a cardboard about three feet long and six or seven inches wide with the word* WELCOME *on it. Each has hold of the cardboard. When they begin, each points to the word* WELCOME.

All: You see this card that we are holding?
           It means a welcome to you all.
           We will tell you of the Savior
           How He saves both great and small.

First: (*Pointing to the first two letters,* WE, *and emphasizing* "We")
           The first two letters of this word
           I know you all can read it,
           We must love the Savior more
           For We surely need it.

Second: (*Pointing to the letter* C, *emphasizing* "Christ")
           The middle letter stands for *Christ,*
           Our Prophet, Priest, and King.
           He came from heaven to save us;
           And of His goodness we will sing.

Third: (*Pointing to the letters* COME, *emphasizing* "Come")
           And do you see the last four letters?
           Come unto me and rest.

33

And all who love and serve Him
Shall be forever blest.

All: We come to Christ today
              To worship and to praise;
              In songs of adoration
              Our voices we will raise.

*(Now the three children sing the first stanza of "I
Love to Tell the Story" changing the pronoun "I" to
"We," thus "We love to tell the story. . . .")*

3. MY LITTLE BIBLE *(For three little girls or boys)*

   (While the children march to the platform the organ
plays very softly the first four lines of "Jesus Loves Me."
*As soon as the organ is silent one of the girls faces the
other two and the dialogue begins. When the last one
begins to speak the organ plays very softly as if coming
from a distance the chorus of "Jesus Loves Me." When
the last one has spoken the organ plays "Jesus Loves Me"
for the children.)*

First: Do you see this little Bible? *(Shows little
              Bible)*
                 I hold it tight within my hand,
              For I do not want to lose it,
                 It is the best book in the land.

Second: Come, let me see that little Bible
                 Of which you seem to think so much.
              I hope it has lots of pictures.
                 It will not hurt it just to touch. *(1st hands
                 Bible to 2nd)*

Third: I'd like to see that Bible too.
              I heard about it, O, so much.

But I hear 'tis not for children.
Just old people and all such. (*2nd hands Bible to 3rd*)

First: Now you are wrong about my Bible.
It is a book for children too.
It has the story of baby Jesus.
Who came from heaven for me and you.

Third: When I looked into this Bible
I read of Jesus' birth
How angels sang a song from heaven
Goodwill to men and peace on earth.

Second: And I read that little children
Jesus took upon His knee.
For they belong now to His kingdom
And there they shall His glory see.

First: I am so glad you love my Bible (*Organ begins to play softly, Jesus Loves Me*)
It is a book for children too.
For this Jesus came to save us
He is now our Savior true.

(*Now the children sing with organ accompaniment:* "*Jesus Loves Me, This I Know*")

4. SAVIOR

(*An acrostic by six children, each having a letter. The star * indicates that the word must be emphasized. The letter must be raised at the time the word is spoken.*)

All: We come to spell a word for you
And tell about each letter.

And when we spell the whole word through
You'll understand it better.

S: When Mary brought the baby Jesus
  To present Him to the Lord
Old SIMEON* came and blessed the Savior
  In accordance with God's Word.

A: And then there came the dear old ANNA.*
  And looked upon the child so fair.
She thanked the Lord for the Redeemer,
  And spake about His glory there.

V: The VIRGIN* Mary heard these blessings
  And wondered what this child would be.
But she believed, as God had promised
  That He would set the sinner free.

I: Yet in the INN* of Bethlehem
  There was no room for the dear stranger.
They sent him out into the street.
  To a stable with a manger.

O: We must have room for this dear Savior
  We must OBEY* our gracious Lord.
Obedience which God will give us,
  Gives room to Him, thus says His Word.

R: Our Savior now is our *REDEEMER.**
  He saves from sin and sets us free.
And with Anna and with Simeon
  We shall His heavenly glory see.

5. HYMN: "No Room in the Inn" (*by class or group*)

No beautiful chamber, No soft cradle bed.
  No place but a manger, No place for His head;

No praises of gladness, No thought of their sin
   No glory but sadness, No room in the inn.

Chorus:

No room, No room for Jesus, Oh give Him welcome free.
Lest ye should hear at heaven's gate.
There is no room for thee.

No sweet consecration, No seeking His part,
   No humiliation, No place in the heart;
No tho't of the Savior, No sorrow for sin,
   No prayer for His favor, No room in the inn.

No one to receive Him. No welcome while here,
   No balm to relieve, no staff but a spear;
No seeking His treasure, No weeping for sin,
   No doing His pleasure, No room in the inn

6. A PRESENT (*By a little child*)

I have a present in my hand;
   I got it just today;
Do you want to see the present?
   Before you go away?

'Tis a book of Bible stories,
   And it has nice pictures too;
But there are so very many;
   I can't show them all to you.

But the one I like the best,
   Now to you I'll show.
'Tis the one of Baby Jesus.
   The Savior, we must know.

(*She now opens book, shows picture, and says*:)

This is Jesus whom I love.
Who came to us from heaven above.

7. CHRISTMAS BELLS

(A bell exercise for five children, each having a paper bell which they swing in unison from left to right as they recite the first and last stanzas in unison.)

All: Ding, Dong; Ding, Dong;
                Christmas bells; Christ is born.
                Ding, Dong; Ding, Dong.
                Christmas bells; Christmas Morn.

(Each in his turn steps forward and recites his stanza and steps back to his place in line upon completing his stanza.)

Third: My bell tells you of the Savior
                Born in Bethlehem one day.
                They laid Him in a humble manger.
                And there He slept upon the hay.

First: My bell tells a wondrous story
                Of angels coming to this earth;
                They told the shepherds the glad story
                Of our Savior's lowly birth.

Fifth: My bell tells how wise men came
                To worship Him and gifts to bring.
                A star had shown to them the place
                Where they could find the newborn king.

Second: My bell rings throughout the ages.
                The gospel bell rings loud and clear.
                Come unto me and find salvation;
                Before the Savior now appear.

Fourth: My bell tells you of the Savior
                Whom we love with all our heart.

We are not ashamed of Jesus,
    Nor from His love will ever part.

All: Ding, Dong; Ding, Dong;
    Christmas bells, Christ is born.
Ding, Dong; Ding, Dong;
    Christmas bells, Christmas Morn.

8. HYMN: "Hark, the Herald Angels Sing"

9. THE GOSPEL MESSAGE (*Recitation*)

On the hills of Bethlehem
    Shepherds watched their flocks by night,
The sky was clear, the weather cold,
    When there appeared a glorious light.

An angel came to comfort them,
    Proclaimed the birth of Christ the King.
"Fear Not," the heavenly angel said,
    "For tidings of great joy I bring.

"For unto you has come a Savior,
    Born in Bethlehem's stable stall.
There you will find the baby sleeping
    In manger bed, a baby small.

"Do not expect a royal garment
    To clothe this humble Savior dear.
For wrapped in swaddling cloth you'll find Him.
    Go now and worship Him in fear."

The shepherds went and found the baby
    As the angels had foretold.
They worshiped Him with joy and gladness,
    Their hearts were filled with joy untold.

They were the first to tell the story
  Of Jesus' birth to others too.
Many came and saw the wonder,
  And believed the story true.

And so the story of salvation
  Must be proclaimed to all the earth.
That every one may see the glory
  The glory of the Savior's birth.

10. UNTO YOU IS BORN THIS DAY A SAVIOR

(*This exercise has four recitations for four groups of four boys or girls each. The first member of each group has a cardboard with the following words on it respectively:* 1. UNTO YOU. 2. IS BORN. 3. THIS DAY. 4. A SAVIOR. *Each member of each group recites one stanza. This exercise can also be given by one group of four boys or girls, or mixed. In that case, each boy or girl carries a card and recites all four stanzas relating to his or her card. All groups go to platform at once. Cards are raised to show the words as the first speaker in each group recites the first line.*)

First Group: UNTO YOU

1. "UNTO YOU is born a Savior."
    Thus the Angels did proclaim
    When they brought the heavenly message,
    Speaking in God's holy name.

2. "UNTO YOU," thus heard the shepherds.
    It was for them the Savior came;
    They went to see the baby Jesus,
    And glorified His holy name.

3. "UNTO YOU," thus heard the sinners,
   All who lived both far and near
   "Unto you I come to save you,
   Listen to my voice and hear."

4. "UNTO YOU" is also spoken
   Unto all of us today.
   Let us seek Him with the shepherds
   And His law let us obey.

Second Group: IS BORN

1. "IS BORN," thus said the heavenly angel,
   Born a child like you and me;
   Born like unto us His brethren;
   And thus He can our Savior be.

2. "IS BORN," and yet He came from heaven,
   Son of God from heaven above.
   He left the heavens and its glory,
   To display the Father's love.

3. "IS BORN" to be our precious Savior.
   Yet found no room in Bethlehem's inn.
   He was despised, by men rejected:
   He bore the burden of our sin.

4. "IS BORN!" O glorious love of God!
   Our salvation now is near.
   Jesus is our Lord and Savior,
   And as our King He did appear.

Third Group: THIS DAY

1. "THIS DAY," the heavenly angel said
   "Is born the Savior of the world.
   Go now and seek Him as your King,
   Let all the banners be unfurled."

2. "THIS DAY," a most important word;
   All todays have been tomorrows,
   All todays pass soon away.
   With their joys and with their sorrows.

3. "THIS DAY" the shepherds went to see,
   They did not wait a single day.
   They left their sheep, and hurried on.
   To see the child without delay.

4. "THIS DAY" if you will hear my voice."
   The Savior calls to us today,
   "Harden not your sinful heart,
   But follow me in every way."

Fourth Group: A SAVIOR

1. "A SAVIOR" shout it through the ages.
   A Savior born to set us free,
   A deliverer from bondage.
   To Him for salvation flee.

2. "A SAVIOR" not just of one country
   Not only of the good and meek.
   But mercy for the greatest sinner,
   For all who will His mercy seek.

3. "A SAVIOR," complete and perfect,
   Through all the ages He is true!
   He saves us from distress and anguish
   Eternally He saves us too.

4. Unto you is born A SAVIOR!
   Give heed to His voice today.
   Harden not your sinful heart
   But follow Him in every way.

(*Now they form two rows of six, and a front row of four showing the words*: UNTO YOU THIS DAY IS

BORN A SAVIOR. *In this position they sing together, "Joy to the World.")*

11. WHO IS THE SAVIOR?

(Dialogue for four boys; with a little change may be used for four girls. Sitting room with table and lamp, four chairs. Big dictionary and Bible with concordance and other books on the table. Henry sits at the table looking up some words in the dictionary.)

Henry: That's some job. Looking up words in the dictionary. And then when you find the word you don't know what to do with it. The first word I must look up is "Savior." I suppose I have to look by "S." Here I have it s-a-b, s-a-l, s-a-r, s-a-w, no that's too far. Here I have it, S-a-v, S-a-v-i-o-r — Savior . . . One who saves.

(Three boys come in)

Dick: Hey there, look at Henry. He is really studying. Look at all these books.

Peter: What are you trying to do?

Henry: Why? Weren't you boys at Sunday School last Sunday?

Peter: Yes, we all were. But what has that to do with all these books, and all that ambition?

Henry: You certainly are forgetful! Don't you remember that our teacher said that we should look up the two words, "Savior" and "Salvation"? We must know the meaning of them.

Dick: O, yes, I remember, but I forgot to do it.

John: So did I.

Peter: So did I.

John: And we are supposed to have it done by next Sunday. Our teacher said that it will help us to understand Christmas better.

Henry: That's what I thought. Come now, you bright fellows! Let us do it together. Four heads are better than one.

Peter: All right. How far did you get?

Henry: Well, I really just started. I found the word "Savior." I will read the definition this dictionary gives and you write it down. This is what it says here: "Savior: Jesus . . . Christ . . . The redeemer: one who saves, or delivers from danger."

Dick: Say, what kind of a dictionary do you have there? Talking of Jesus Christ and redeemer. I never heard of a dictionary like that. It sounds like a Christian dictionary or Bible dictionary to me.

Henry: It is just a common Webster's Dictionary. But what else could it say? Savior really means Jesus. He *is* the Savior. He is the Redeemer. He really saves from the danger of being lost forever. But say, isn't it wonderful that even in a common dictionary, where everybody can read it, it tells us that Jesus is the Savior.

John: I can hardly believe it. But I am going to remember that. Now, what is the next word? What was it again? "Salvation"?

Henry: That's right. No where we are. S-a-l, S-a-l-v-a-t-i o-n — "Salvation: The act of saving, preservation from destruction, rescue, spiritual delivery from sin and death."

Dick: Well, I certainly never knew that Webster's Dictionary would speak of spiritual delivery from sin and death. I wonder if Webster was a Christian.

Henry: I don't know. But even if he wasn't, he couldn't have said it any different. The words "Savior" and "salvation" do not fit anywhere else but by Jesus who is the true Savior. There is no other Savior than Jesus.

Peter: And so it is with Salvation. Jesus the Savior brings Salvation. No one else can deliver us from sin and death. And that is just why we celebrate Christmas. I will use my dictionary more for my Bible terms.

John: But isn't there something else we have to do for our next week's lesson?

Dick: Yes, but I don't remember much of it. We had to look up in some book where the first time the word "Savior" is mentioned in the Old Testament. And then we have to do the same thing in the New Testament. But where will you find that?

John: That's easy enough. Suppose we each take a Bible. I will look through Genesis, Dick will look though Exodus, and so forth. Then we ought to find the first time the word "Savior" is used in the Bible.

Henry: Yes, we could; but how long do you think that would take us? But teacher said to look it up in a concordance.

Peter: A concordance? What is that? I never heard of it.

John: I remember now. Lat year I had to find a text and I couldn't find it anywhere. At last my father said "Look it up in a Bible with a concordance." And there in the back of the Bible were many helps and there was also a concordance. And in just a couple of minutes I found my text.

Dick: I would like to see such a book.

Henry: Why, here it is, right in this Bible. Just look. (*All look*) Every important word of the Bible is in it. Now take the word "Savior." Here it is. And here are all the places where that word is found. It is found (*Counts out loud*) fifteen times in the Old Testament, and (*Counts*) twenty-four times in the New Testament.

Peter: Say, that's fine. I never looked in the back of my Bible. Now we have to look up these places, and then we are done.

Henry: The first time the word Savior is used is in II Samuel 22:3: "God is my rock . . . and the horn of my salvation. My high tower and my refuge, my savior. Thou savest me from violence."

Dick: What do you know about that! Savior and salvation are both found in that text!

Henry: Yes, and did you notice that God is here called the Savior, and so it is in all the texts in the Old Testament. God saves and He is our salvation.

John: (*Poised to copy*) Now what does that concordance say is the first text in the New Testament with the word Savior?

Henry: Well, who can guess?

Dick: I think I know. The angels said to the shepherds: "Unto you is born this day in the city of David, a Savior.

Henry: I am glad that you know that text. But it is not the first; it is the second. The first we find in Luke 1:47, in the Hymn of Mary, "My spirit rejoiced in God the Savior." Here God is still mentioned as Savior. But as soon as Christ is born then the angels call Jesus the Savior, and then all New Testament texts speak of Jesus as the Savior.

John: Say, I'm glad we came here. From now on I'll use my

dictionary and the concordance more in my Bible study. I've learned something today.

Henry: I think we will be better able to celebrate Christmas. Jesus is the only Savior to bring salvation to us.

John: Well, I think we can go home now. I want to make a better copy of the text and of the definitions we found.

Dick: Well, this is one time we will be prepared for our Sunday School. Thanks to Henry. I am also going to use the dictionary and concordance more. And above all I am going to use the Bible more.

John: So am I. In this way we will serve our Savior better. Good night, Henry!

Henry: (*While clearing table*) Good night boys. See you Sunday.

All: Good Night, and, Merry Christmas.

12. GOODNIGHT (*By three small girls. The tallest one speaks first.*)

> Again the feast of Christmas
> Speeds on toward its end.
> In speaking and in singing
> This day is nearly spent.
>
> We thank you for your presence
> Your kindness and your cheer.
> We gave to you this program
> With love and hearts sincere.
>
> And as we now go homeward,
> May God His blessings send.
> And may the light of Christmas
> Now spread throughout the land.

1st little girl: Good night, everybody!

3rd little girl: Come back next year — Good night.

> — Program prepared and arranged by
> Andrew De Vries
> Used with permission of the
> Midwest Sunday School Association

7. WE TELL THE STORY

Suggestions. Songs throughout may be sung by individual or combined classes or choirs, depending upon the organization presenting the program, or the breadth of participation desired.

PRELUDE: (*Organ or piano*)

PROCESSIONAL: "O Little Town of Bethlehem"

PRAYER:

WELCOME: "Our Greeting Is a Carol" (*Four small children*)

    First: We want to give a greeting

    Second: It is not very long.

    Third: We're happy at this meeting

    Fourth: We'll welcome you with song.

NARRATION: "Jesus Our Savior" (*By four children seated in a semi-circle. An Intermediate or Junior pupil to represent Mother and Primary pupils as children.*)

Mother: Children! It's almost time to go to bed. Tomorrow we go to church to hear the story of Christ's birth and to take part in the program. After that we will go to Grandmother's house.

First Child: Tommorow is Jesus' birthday. How long ago was He born?

Mother: A long, long time ago — more than nineteen hundred years ago.

Second Child: How I wish I had been a little child then. I could have seen the baby Jesus.

Mother: Yes, that would have been nice. But the little Jewish boys and girls did not know Jesus as you do.

Third Child: Why not, mother?

Mother: They did not have a complete Bible like we have. Their scribes and leaders read only the law and the prophets, like we have in the Old Testament. They did have the prophecies of Christ's coming. They knew He was coming and were waiting. You remember that after God created Adam and Eve and placed them in the garden, Satan entered into the heart of man. It was against this dark background of sin that God gave the first promise. In Genesis 3:15 we read, "And I will put enmity between thee and the woman, and between thy seed and her seed; it shall bruise thy head, and thou shalt bruise his heel."

This was the first definite announcement that the Messiah would come. This promise was repeated to Noah, Abraham, Isaac, Jacob, and others. All the while the people were waiting for the promise to be fulfilled. God gave them prophets who were inspired by Him to write concerning the coming of the Messiah. Upon the first promise were based all the others.

PROPHECIES: (*Two or more readers, preferably out of sight with a microphone; can also be presented by a Speaking Choir*)

First Reader: Genesis 49:10, "The scepter shall not depart from Judah, nor the lawgiver from between his feet, until Shiloh come, and unto him shall the gathering of the people be."

Second Reader: Numbers 24:17, "There shall come a Star out of Jacob, and a Scepter shall rise out of Israel."

First Reader: Isaiah 9:6, "For unto us a child is born, unto us a son is given; and the government shall be upon His shoulder: and his name shall be called; Wonderful, Counsellor, the Mighty God, the Everlasting Father, the Prince of Peace."

Second Reader: Jeremiah 23:5, "Behold the days come, saith

the Lord, that I will raise unto David a righteous Branch, and a King shall reign and prosper, and shall execute judgment and justice in the earth."

First Reader: Isaiah 11:1, "And there shall come forth a rod out of the stem of Jesse, and a branch shall grow out of his roots."

Second Reader: Micah 5:2, "But thou, Bethlehem, though thou be little among the thousands of Judah, yet out of thee shall he come forth unto me that is to be ruler in Israel; whose goings forth have been from of old from everlasting."

Mother: After the last prophet, Malachi, God did not speak to His people for about four hundred years, and the people still waited. This is as much of the Bible as the Jewish children had. We have the prophecy and its fulfillment.

INSTRUMENTAL MUSIC: "Silent Night" (*May also be sung by a class or chorus*)

Mother: But there came a time when God spoke again. It was in the days of Herod when Zacharias was priest in the temple at Jerusalem, that the angel Gabriel came to him and said, "Fear not Zacharias, for thy prayer is heard and thy wife Elizabeth shall bear thee a son, and thou shalt call his name John. And thou shalt have joy and gladness; and many shall rejoice at His birth. For he shall be great in the sight of the Lord, and he shall be filled with the Holy Ghost, even from his mother's womb. And many of the children of Israel shall he turn to the Lord their God. And he shall go before him in the spirit and power of Elias, to turn the hearts of the fathers to the children, and the disobedient to the wis-

dom of the just; to make ready a people prepared for the
Lord."

He was not the Messiah but the messenger who would
go before Him. After six months the angel Gabriel was
sent to Mary, a virgin, who was to marry Joseph. And
the angel said "Behold, thou shalt bring forth a Son and
shall call his name Jesus. He shall be great, and shall be
called the Son of the Highest and he shall reign over
the house of Jacob forever. And of his kingdom there
shall be no end." This was to be the long-awaited Messiah, but the people did not yet know.

SOLO: "O Holy Night" (*May also be sung by a class or
chorus*)

Mother: The town of Bethlehem was crowded with people
because Caesar ordered a decree for a census to be taken.
All families were required to go to the place of their
birth. "And Joseph also went up into the city of David,
which is called Bethlehem; to be taxed with Mary his
espoused wife, being great with child. And so it was,
that, while they were there, the days were accomplished
that she should be delivered. And she brought forth her
first born son, and wrapped him in swaddling clothes,
and laid him in a manger, because there was no room
for them in the Inn."

RECITATION: "There Was No Room"
            Doors were shut against Him then,
            The only room, a cattle pen,
            The only light, a star above,
            The only warmth, a mother's love.

Mother: Not far from Bethlehem was the beautiful country
of Judea with its many steep mountains and gently roll-
ing hills. The moon was casting a soft light, and the

sky was radiant with countless twinkling stars, illuminating the field where flocks of sheep lay sleeping under the watchful eye of their shepherds.

SONG: "While Shepherds Watched Their Flocks by Night"

Mother: "And suddenly there was with the angel a multitude of the heavenly host, praising God and saying, 'Glory to God in the highest, and on earth peace, good will toward men.' "

SONGS: "Hark, the Herald Angels Sing"; "Joy to the World"

Mother: The shepherds stood listening with awe to the multitude of the heavenly host praising God. And after they had gone away from them into heaven, the shepherds said one to another, "We must see this thing which is come to pass which the Lord hath made known to us. Let us now go even unto Bethlehem."

EXERCISE: "O Little Town of Bethlehem" (*Nine children*)

1. Best gift that ever came to earth,
   You gave us in the Saviour's birth,
   O little town of Bethlehem.

2. Ever since the manger bed
   A halo hovers round your head,
   O little town of Bethlehem.

3. Though you are now a city old
   Still is your precious story told,
   O little town of Bethlehem.

4. Heaven and earth in thee once met
   And the glory lingers yet,
   O little town of Bethlehem.

5. Like the star of long ago
   You cast across the years a glow
   O little town of Bethlehem.

6. Even though you're far away
   You seem so near on Christmas Day,
   O little town of Bethlehem.

7. Happily of thee we sing
   As the birthplace of our King,
   O little town of Bethlehem.

8. Ever we will faithful be
   To the one who came to thee,
   O little town of Bethlehem.

9. Mankind needs the heavenly Stranger
   Born within your lowly manger,
   O little town of Bethlehem.

Mother: We read in Luke 2:15, "And the shepherds came with haste and found Mary and Joseph, and the babe lying in a manger."

SONG: "Away in a Manger"

Mother: The shepherds praised God for all the things that had been seen and heard, but Mary kept all these sayings in her heart. After the shepherds were gone, wise men from the East came to Jerusalem asking "Where is he born king of the Jews? For we have seen his star in the east and are come to worship him. . . . And, lo, the star which they had seen in the East, went before them, till it came and stood over the place where the young child was." They rejoiced with exceeding great joy when they saw the Star again.

INSTRUMENTAL MUSIC: "Star of the East" (*May be vocal*)

Mother: The wise men worshipped the young child and brought gifts worthy of a King.
This is the story of Jesus' birth. But the Bible tells us more about Jesus our Savior.

SONG: "Stranger of Galilee" (*May be instrumental or vocal*)

Mother: Jesus grew in stature and increased in wisdom and in favor with God and man. He was obedient to Mary and Joseph. When he was about thirty years old, He began teaching the disciples and the multitudes. He healed the sick and raised the dead. He also took little children in His arms and blessed them and said, "Suffer the little children to come unto me, and forbid them not for of such is the kingdom of Heaven."
This Jesus who loves little children, loved us enough to be willing to suffer and die for our sins, that we might be saved. But rose again and ascended into Heaven and is there now making intercession for us and will soon come again. When Jesus was on earth the people did not know Him. If we know Jesus as our wonderful Savior don't you think we should tell other's about Him? Jesus said in John 20:24, "As the Father hath sent me, even so send I you."

ORGAN: "So Send I You"

Mother: Won't you pray that as you grow older you may answer that call to tell others about our Savior who is truly our Beautiful Savior? Won't you sing with us "Beautiful Savior"?

SONG: "Beautiful Saviour" (*Joined by entire audience*)

FAREWELL: "A Closing Wish"

We've had a happy hour,
Or so it seems to me;
And I believe we've learned a lot,
Now, friends, don't you agree?

I think perhaps we realize,
A little more today
How good our God has been to us
In every kind of way.

I do not know a better way
This time we could have spent,
I think that we can all go home
Quite happy and content.

So, since our program now is done
That's what I hope you'll do
And best of Christmas wishes, friends,
Please take along with you.

—With Permission of the
Overisel Christian Reformed Church

8. THE CHRISTMAS STORY

(While children assemble on platform organ plays soft background music: "O Holy Night, The Stars Are Brightly Shining." Children softly hum along as they take up their places. Then music fades out.)

(Organ plays "O Little Town of Bethlehem" softly as select group speaks in unison;)

> O little town of Bethlehem,
> How still we see thee lie!
> Above thy deep and dreamless sleep
> The silent stars go by.

(*Background music picks up the rest of the song and completes one stanza. The music fades out.*)

Narrator: "And it came to pass in those days, that there went out a decree from Caesar Augustus that all the world should be taxed. And all went to be taxed, everyone into his own city. And Joseph also went up from Galilee, out of the city of Nazareth into Judea, unto the city of David, which is called Bethlehem, because he was of the house and lineage of David: to be taxed with Mary his wife, who expected a child."

(*Organ plays a stanza of "O Little Town of Bethlehem," playing with emphasis the final two lines:*)

> The hope and fears of all the years
> Are met in thee tonight.

Narrator: "And so it was, that while they were there the days were accomplished that Mary should be delivered. And she brought forth her firstborn son, and wrapped him in swaddling clothes, and laid him in a manger, because there was no room for them in the inn."

(*Group sings: "Silent Night, Holy Night"*)

(*Background music repeats the last strains of "Silent Night"*)

(*Organ plays softly "O Holy Night" while select group speaks in unison:*)

O holy night, the stars are brightly shining,
It is the night of the dear Savior's birth.
Long lay the world in sin and error pining.
Till He appeared and the soul felt His worth.
For yonder breaks a new and glorious morn. . . .

(*Organ music completes song with emphasis*)

Narrator: "And there were in the same country, shepherds abiding in the field, keeping watch over their flock by night."

(*Group sings:*)

How silently, how silently
The wondrous gift is given
So God imparts to human hearts
The blessings of his heaven.
No ear may hear his coming
But in the world of sin
Where meek souls will receive Him,
Still the Christchild enters in.

Narrator: "And lo, the angel of the Lord came upon them, and the glory of the Lord shone round about them and they were sore afraid. And the angel said unto them,"

(*During the above reading, organ plays softly the first four lines of:*)

While shepherds watched their flocks by night
All seated on the ground.

The angel of the Lord came down,
And glory shone around.

(*Then with emphasis, organ plays and group sings:*)

Fear not, said he, for mighty dread
Had seized their troubled minds.
Glad tidings of great joy I bring
To you and all mankind.

To you in David's town this day
Is born in David's line
A Saviour who is Christ the Lord.
And this shall be the sign:
The heavenly babe you there shall find
All meanly wrapped in swaddling bands
And in a manger laid.

(*Organ makes transition, then accompanies small children as they sing "Away in a Manger"*)

Narrator: "And suddenly there was with the angel, a multitude of the heavenly host, praising God and saying:"

(*Group sings: "Joy to the World"*)

Narrator: "And it came to pass as the angels were gone away from them into heaven, the shepherds said one to another,"

(*Select group recites in unison:*)

Angels we have heard on high
Sweetly singing o'er the plains.
And the mountains in reply
Echoing their joyous strains.

(*Group sings: "Gloria in excelsis Deo"*)

(*Select group recites in unison:*)

> Come to Bethlehem and see
> Him whose birth the angels sing.
> Come adore on bended knee
> Christ the Lord the newborn King.

(*Group sings: "Gloria in excelsis Deo"*)

Narrator: "Behold there came wise men from the east to Jerusalem, saying: Where is he that is born King of the Jews? For we have seen his star in the east, and have come to worship him."

(*Group sings:*)

> We three kings of Orient are,
> Bearing gifts we traverse afar.
> Field and fountain, moor and mountain
> Following yonder star.

> *Chorus:*
> O star of wonder, star of night,
> Star with royal beauty bright,
> Westward leading, still proceeding,
> Guide us to thy perfect light.

Narrator: "And when they were come into the house, they saw the young child with Mary his mother. And they fell down and worshipped him; and then they opened their treasures."

First Speaker: Born a King on Bethlehem's plain
> Gold I bring to crown Him again
> King forever, ceasing never
> Over us all to reign.

Second Speaker: Frankincense to offer have I,
> Incense owns a deity nigh

> Prayer and praising, all men raising
> Worship Him, God most high.

Third Speaker: Myrrh is mine, its bitter perfume
> Breathes a life of gathering gloom
> Sorrowing, sighing, bleeding, dying,
> Sealed in the stone-cold tomb.

(During the above organ softly plays chorus through once then group sings last stanza and chorus:)

> Glorious now behold him rise
> King and God and sacrifice
> Alleluia, alleluia,
> Earth to heaven replies.

Chorus:

> O star of wonder, star of night,
> Star of royal beauty bright
> Westward leading, still proceeding,
> Guide us to the perfect light.

Narrator: And the shepherds returned glorifying and praising God for all the things that they had seen and heard.

(Group sings first stanza of "O Come, All Ye Faithful")

(Children file from platform as they and entire audience sing the second and third stanza of "O Come, All Ye Faithful")

—John Vriesinga

9. THE BIRTHDAY OF A KING

The following unit can be used effectively in a number of different ways. A few phrases or expressions in the story will have to be altered to adapt it to the several possible uses.

The carols can be sung by a hidden choir. The story may be told by a teen-age girl. Seated in a rocker, she tells the story to a child from the nursery seated close at her side. A lapel microphone makes it possible for all to hear her clearly.

The scene can also be that of a teacher telling the story to her Sunday School class seated on the platform, with the class singing the carols.

Another alternative is to have the entire Sunday School, a department, a class, or select group on the platform sing the carols while a narrator, with microphone, to the side or out of sight tells the story.

SONG: "Hark! the Herald Angels Sing"

NARRATOR: Did you hear that song, my child? Come and sit here close beside me and I will tell you the story of that first Christmas.

When you came to live with us we were all very happy. Mother sang a song of thanksgiving in her heart for your birth; but when Jesus was born, angels sang. They sang on high, telling to the world that Christ was born. Mary and Joseph had come to Bethlehem by the order of the government to be taxed, and they had traveled many days. It was a tiresome and difficult trip for Mary. Coming to Bethlehem, they sought a place to stay. They went here and there, but every place was taken, for many people had arrived before them. Finally, a kind innkeeper offered them the only place he had left, the Stable.

God has told us in His Word, many years before this, that He would send a Saviour into the world. After Adam and Eve disobeyed in the garden of Eden, God promised a Saviour, born of a woman, to redeem His people from their sin. Isaiah, the prophet, spoke of this promise when he declared, "For unto us a Child is born, unto us a son is given, and the government shall be upon his shoulder and his name shall be called Wonderful, Counsellor, Mighty God, Everlasting Father, Prince of Peace."

The prophet Micah told us the name of the city where Christ was born: "But you, O Bethlehem Ephrathah, who are little to be among the tribes of Judah, from you shall come forth for me one who is to be ruler in Israel, whose origin is from of old, from everlasting."

SONG: "Oh! Little Town of Bethlehem"

NARRATOR: Now during the night, Mary gave birth to her baby, the Son of God. She did not have a lovely crib to place her baby in. She wrapped him in swaddling clothes and lay him in a manger.

SONG: "Away in a Manger" (*May also be sung by the Mother who tells the story, or by someone else as a solo*)

NARRATOR: "Now when Jesus was born in Bethlehem of Judea in the days of Herod the king, behold there came wise men from the east to Jerusalem saying, Where is he that is born King of the Jews? for we have seen his star in the east and are come to worship him.

"The star, which they saw in the east, went before them, till it came and stood over where the young child was. And when they were come into the house, they saw the young child with Mary his mother, and fell down, and worshiped him. And they opened their treasures and presented unto him gifts, gold and frankincense, and myrrh."

God did not tell Herod the King, in Jerusalem, that Jesus was to be born in Bethlehem, but he did tell the shepherds who were keeping watch over their flocks on the plains of Judea, when the angel of the Lord came upon them and the glory of the Lord shone round about them and they were sore afraid. And suddenly there was with the angel a multitude of angels, and this is what they said, "Glory to God in the highest and on earth peace, good-will toward men."

This, dear, is one of the beautiful choruses that Handel has put to music in his oratorio, "The Messiah." Let us all sing together the song, "While Shepherds Watched Their Flocks by Night."

SONG: "While Shepherds Watched Their Flocks by Night"

NARRATOR: Now before very many days had passed, the parents of Jesus brought him to the temple to do for him after the custom of the law. Then the devout Simeon, who was waiting in the temple, took him up in his arms and blessed God and said: "Lord, now lettest thou thy servant depart in peace, according to thy word: For mine eyes have seen thy salvation, which thou hast prepared before the face of all people; a light to lighten the Gentiles, and the glory of thy people Israel." And Joseph and his mother marvelled at those things which were spoken of him. And Simeon blessed them, and said unto Mary, his mother, "Behold, this child is set for the fall and rising again of many in Israel; and for a sign which shall be spoken against; (Yea, a sword shall pierce through thy own soul also) that the thoughts of many hearts may be revealed."

The days of peace and happiness for Mary and Joseph and the boy Jesus were short, for soon they had to flee for their lives, for Herod sought to kill the young child.

Thus began a life of suffering for His people. "He was despised and rejected of men, a man of sorrows and acquainted with grief."

It is our sin and our disobedience that had caused Him so much suffering. Nevertheless, He was obedient even unto death. And He gave His life a ransom for many. He would have us obey His great commission and tell it unto others.

SONG: "We've a Story to Tell to the Nations" (*Sung with enthusiastic jubilation*)

NARRATOR: And so, my dear, we are to be His messengers, telling men everywhere the good news of the Saviour's birth.

SONG:

Go tell it on the mountains,
Over the hills and everywhere;
Go tell it on the mountains,
That Jesus Christ is born.

—Bertha Yff
By permission of
The Young Calvinist Federation

10. THE BABE AT BETHLEHEM

General Outline:

1. Approximately twenty to forty children to form the choral group to sing the carols.

2. A cast of ten children — Mary, Joseph, five Shepherds, and three Wise Men.

3. A narrator — a teacher or older pupil — to read the story.

Properties:

1. Ten housecoats reaching to the floor for the cast.

2. Seven suitable head pieces for the shepherds, Mary and Joseph.

3. Three crowns and three suitable jars for Wise Men.

4. A cradle filled with straw and small chair for Mary at front center of stage.

5. A microphone far to one side for narrator.

6. Song sheets with carols in the order they are to be sung, for the choral group.

Suggestions:

One teacher should be given excerpts of the text coming before each card and be responsible for starting the singing at the appropriate moment.

Another teacher should be given texts before entrances and be responsible for characters entering at right moment.

To these two teachers goes the responsibility for success or failure of the program as success lies in smooth timing. The program should flow smoothly and long pauses avoided.

Also it is necessary to practice as many times as possible. One Sunday School practiced one school period just singing and two whole periods the entire program.

A good effect is achieved by lighting only the front stage, leaving the audience without light or in dim light.

SONG: "It Came upon a Midnight Clear" (*First stanza*)

NARRATOR: "And in the sixth month the angel Gabriel was sent from God unto a city of Galilee, named Nazareth, to a virgin espoused to a man whose name was

Joseph, of the house of David, and the virgin's name was Mary.

"And the angel said unto her, Fear not, Mary, for thou hast found favour with God.

"And, behold thou shalt conceive in thy womb, and bring forth a son, and shalt call his name Jesus.

"He shall be great and shall be called the Son of the Highest. And it came to pass in those days, that there went out a decree from Caesar Augustus, that all the world should be taxed.

"And all went to be taxed, every one into his own city."

(*Enter Mary and Joseph. Mary is seated at the cradle and Joseph stands at her side.*)

NARRATOR: "And Joseph also went up from Galilee, out of the city of Nazareth, into Judaea, unto the city of David, which is called Bethlehem.

"To be taxed with Mary his espoused wife, being great with child."

SONG: "O Little Town of Bethlehem"

NARRATOR: "And so it was, that, while they were there the days were accomplished that she should be delivered."

SONG: "Away in a Manger" (*Hummed while narrator continues*)

NARRATOR: "And she brought forth her firstborn son, and wrapped him in swaddling clothes, and laid him in a manger; because there was no room for them in the inn." (*Narrator waits for humming to end before continuing:*) "And there were in the same country shepherds abiding in the field, keeping watch over their flock by night."

SONG: "Noel" (*Sung once through completely. Then the song is hummed while narrator continues. The chorus is sung after narrator completes the following:*)

NARRATOR: "And, lo, the angel of the Lord came upon them, and the glory of the Lord shone round about them: and they were sore afraid.

"And the angel said unto them, Fear not: for behold, I bring you good tidings of great joy, which shall be to all people.

"For unto you is born this day in the city of David a Savior, which is Christ the Lord." (*This should be timed so that the choir comes in singing the chorus of "Noel" as the reader finishes.*)

"And this shall be a sign unto you, Ye shall find the babe wrapped in swaddling clothes, lying in a manger.

"And suddenly there was with the angel a multitude of the heavenly host praising God, and saying,

"Glory to God in the highest, and on earth peace, good will toward men."

SONG: "While Shepherds Watched Their Flocks by Night"

(*Enter shepherds and stand at the side of the cradle*)

NARRATOR: "And it came to pass, as the angels were gone away from them into heaven, the shepherds said one to another, Let us now go even unto Bethlehem, and see this thing which is come to pass, which the Lord has made known to us.

"And they came with haste, and found Mary and Joseph, and the babe lying in a manger.

"And when they had seen it, they made known abroad the saying which was told them concerning this child. And all they that heard it wondered at those things which were told them by the shepherds. But Mary kept all these things and pondered them in her heart.

"And the shepherds returned, glorifying and praising God for all the things that they had heard and seen, as it was told unto them."

(*Exit shepherds*)

SONG: "O Come, All Ye Faithful"

NARRATOR: "Now when Jesus was born in Bethlehem . . . behold there came wise men from the east to Jerusalem,

"Saying, Where is he that is born King of the Jews? for we have seen his star in the east and are come to worship him.

"When Herod the king had heard these things, he was troubled, and all Jerusalem with him.

"And when he had gathered all the chief priests and scribes of the people together, he demanded of them where Christ should be born.

"And they said unto him, In Bethlehem of Judaea: for thus it is written by the prophet,

"And thou Bethlehem, in the land of Juda, art not the least among the princes of Juda: for out of thee shall come a Governor, that shall rule my people Israel.

"Then Herod, when he had called the wise men, inquired of them diligently what time the star appeared.

"And he sent them to Bethlehem, and said, Go and search diligently for the young child; and when ye have found him, bring me word again, that I may come and worship him also.

"When they had heard the king, they departed; and lo, the star which they saw in the east went before them, till it came and stood over where the young child was."

(*Enter Wise Men, and set jars before the cradle.*)

SONG: "We Three Kings of Orient Are"

NARRATOR: "And when they saw the young child with Mary his mother, they fell down and worshiped him: and when they had opened their treasures, they presented unto him gifts; gold, and frankincense, and myrrh.

"And the wise men being warned of God in a dream, that they should not return to Herod, they departed into their own country another way."

(*Narrator pauses. Exit Wise Men*)

"And when they were departed, behold, the angel of the Lord appeareth to Joseph in a dream, saying, Arise, and take the young child and his mother, and flee into Egypt, and be thou there until I bring thee word, for Herod will seek the young child to destroy him."

(*Exit Mary and Joseph*)

NARRATOR: "When he arose, he took the young child and his mother by night and departed into Egypt.

"And was there until the death of Herod: that it might be fulfilled which was spoken of the Lord by the prophet, saying, Out of Egypt have I called my son."

SONG: "Joy to the World"

— Sunday School at
Milford, Canada

11. THE *TRUE* MEANING OF CHRISTMAS DAY

Suggestions. Girls' teams must recite clearly and in unison. This will add greatly to effect, while bad timing will destroy same. Boys must be clear speakers of about the same age and height. Narrator must be chosen carefully and if possible be furnished a microphone.

ORGAN: (*Plays "Silent Night" while pupils take their places on platform. Chorus of boys and girls in background, four teams of two speakers each in front of chorus. One boy in front center, as Narrator, delivers the prologue and final address.*)

CHORUS: Stanza 1 of "Silent Night" (*Softly*).

PROLOGUE: (*By narrator. To be spoken slowly, carefully, and with feeling, after announcing title.*)

The *True* Meaning of Christmas Day

To us there comes each year at Christmas time,
The pagan meaning of this day.
Of old St. Nick and Santa Claus we hear.
Commercialized exchange of gifts holds sway.
The world perverts the meaning of this day. (*pause*)

We also hear the story of Christ's birth,
The angel's song — The shepherds in the night,
The journey of the wise men from the east.
But — let us pause and seek for further light,
That we may know and love this day aright. (*pause*)

And so the question comes to you and me,
What think we of the Christchild? of the Christ?

FIRST TEAM: (*Two girls now recite in unison the first stanza of the poem. As they begin speaking [loudly and clearly] the organist [and perhaps violins] play "Silent Night," very softly and not too fast.*)

What think ye of this child who lay,
In manger rude, in swaddling clothes arrayed?
So long foretold, the Christchild came to earth,
And awe-struck shepherds heard the angels sing.
They heard the words, "A Savior has been born."
Straightway they went, and seeking made it known,
The saying which was told them of the child.

SECOND TEAM: (*When the first team finishes, the second team [of boys] recites in union Stanza 2. Musical accompaniment continues.*)

And wise men came and brought unto the Babe,
Their gifts of gold, frankincense, and myrrh.
And warned by God, departed by a way not known to
   Herod.
Then in wrath King Herod ordered slain, all babes of
   two years old and under.
From Bethlehem and all the coast thereof, a cry
Of weeping and of mourning then was heard. (*pause*)
But Joseph fled to Egypt with the child;
Forewarned of God, who careth for His own
Better by far than earthly father can.
To Nazareth, in Galilee He comes
In God's own time, the Scriptures to fulfill,
Which say, "He shall be called a Nazarene."

(*If possible the music shall be timed to end very softly just a bit later than the speaking. In any case it should be played to its natural end and not break off abruptly.*)

NARRATOR: "And thou shalt call His name *Jesus;* for He shall save His people from their *sins.*"
   (*and then asks*)
   And so the question comes to you and me, "What think we of the Christchild?"

THIRD TEAM: (*Two girls now recite Stanza 3. Organ (and violins) play softly "The Old Rugged Cross" or "Calvary."*

What think *ye?* What think *ye* of this babe?
What think ye of His coming to this earth?
He who knew no sin
He took upon Himself our sinful human nature,
And satisfaction for our sins He made.
A life of suffering was His
And mocked and ridiculed was He,
And spat upon the scourged and crucified! !
From manger to the grave He bore for us
The wrath of God. In meek humility
The birth of Jesus pointed to the cross,
The path of Jesus led to Calvary.

FOURTII TEAM: (*Two boys now speak and as they reach the words "But lo, the stone is rolled away," the organ [and violins] changes to "Up from the grave He arose." This is played slightly louder and the speakers must raise their voices accordingly. Organist finishes naturally as after Stanza 2.*)

Both *you* and *I* should witness then today;
Nor be ashamed, nor weary of the tale,
Beyond the manger and beyond the cross, we see
The *tomb.* (*Pause*)

But *lo !* the stone is rolled away!
The Christ, so lowly born, hath vic'try won!
The Babe of Bethlehem is King Supreme! !
Ascending to the throne of God on high.

CHORUS: (*After a dramatic pause the organist now plays a chord, then the chorus sings the last stanza of the*

hymn, *"I Know Whom I Have Believed," with special
emphasis on the chorus*)

> I know not when my Lord may come,
> At night or noonday fair,
> Nor if I walk the vale with Him,
> Or meet Him in the air.

> *Chorus*:

> But "I know whom I have believed,
> And am persuaded that He is able
> To keep that which I've committed
> Unto Him against that day."

NARRATOR: *All is again hushed while the boy in center
advances in front of all and speaks the last stanza of the
poem (very slowly and distinctly.)*

> Do you your homage bring to Him just now?
> Is Jesus King in your own life today?

(*Louder*)   For He shall come again

(*Pause*)   this time upon the clouds of heaven

(*Faster*)   in majesty! with trumpet shout!
> in power! in might! In glory He shall reign!

(*Softer*)   And all the Kings of earth shall bow to Him

(*Slower*)   The King of Kings, the *Babe* of Bethlehem.

> — Otto Heerdt

12. PHOEBE'S CHRISTMAS EVE

(A Christmas Playlet for Girls)

Cast:

1. Phoebe, a little girl who dreams, aged about ten to twelve
2. Phoebe's Mother
3. Agatha, twelve to fourteen
4. Dorothy, twelve
5. Ruth, eleven to thirteen
6. A stranger, a Christmas Angel, aged about sixteen
7. Group of Carolers. May be a special choir or various Sunday School Classes in succession.

Scene:

A humble room in which Phoebe lives. (Names may be changed as desired.) The fire, before which she sits wrapped in an old comforter, is nearly out. Over the fire place hangs a gay calendar or the picture of an angel. There is a window at the back center, a door to the right of it. A plain kitchen table completely covered with an old cloth, stands beneath the window. A candle sprite is hidden under the table. If it is not possible to have a window, one may be effectively represented by hanging sash curtains on a rod at the proper height against the wall. An oblong of dark blue paper behind them will give the perfect illusion of a window. (Make the setting as simple or detailed as desired.)

(*The rising curtain shows Phoebe resting in a large but much-worn, deep-cushioned chair. After a wait of about one minute Phoebe's mother enters.*)

Mother: Are you comfortable, dear?

Phoebe: Yes, mother, quite comfortable.

Mother: It breaks my heart to leave you alone after dark, and especially tonight — Christmas Eve.

Phoebe: Oh, I don't mind, mother, very much. When you are gone I imagine all kinds of things to pass away the time.

Mother: You're a brave little girl! The extra work they have given me to do tonight will buy food for us and maybe a bit extra to celebrate our Christmas. I may be late coming home. Perhaps I should tuck you in before I go.

Phoebe: Please, mother, I'd rather sit up here in my chair. My back is very comfortable against the pillow, and it is not nearly so lonely here where I can watch the fire and the angel on the calendar. Isn't she lovely!

Mother: Very well, Phoebe. Sit up if it will make you happier. But I surely wish I could stay with you.

Phoebe: Why doesn't anyone ever come over to play with me, mother? I see the children going by to school every day, and they talk and laugh and seem so happy; but none of them ever come in to talk to me though I smile at them through the window. Why don't they, mother?

Mother: Perhaps they don't know that you would like to have them. I know how lonely it is for you. Keep on being brave, Phoebe. I would like to give you all the things which you should have — proper food to make you strong, and the doll and teddy bear you want so much.

Phoebe: I saw a little girl pass by one day carrying a teddy bear as big as this.

Mother: (*Half to herself*) Why are we so poor? Why must my little one be left without companionship when all around are children who might play with her?

Phoebe: But we are happy, aren't we, mother? Even if you must work, and my back is lame.

Mother: (*With a smile and sigh*) Yes, dear, we are happy. (*Puts on her coat and hat*)

Phoebe: Agatha and Dorothy went by this afternoon with great big bundles in their arms. I thought they were going to stop, but they never even looked up at my window. They are rich, aren't they mother, and are always so busy. They go to school, and they learn to sing and play the piano. Still, they used to come here once in a while. Wonder why they never come anymore?

Mother: There seems to be a great gulf between wealth and poverty that is seldom crossed, daughter. Their mother and I used to go to school together. But she married a man who had a great deal of money, while I was left without your father very soon after you were born. So I have to work to take care of my little girl. But there! On Christmas Eve we must smile and think of God's greatest gift to men.

Phoebe: Of course we must, and I am glad that for Him there is no difference between rich and poor.

Mother: Now I'll put your glass of milk close by. It will help you get well. Cuddle up now in your blankets. Good bye, dear. I'll hurry and get home as early as I can.

Phoebe: Please put that little candle in the window, mother. It reminds me of the Christchild and the star to lighten the way of the Wise Men to Jesus. Good bye, Mumsie, I'll be very good; I'll play that Angelina is a brand new doll. (*Exit mother. Phoebe rocks battered old doll in her arms.*) You are very plain, Angelina. Maybe that is why some little girl threw you away. But never mind; I am plain too, and I'm glad Mumsie found you and brought you to me. Your back is straight and strong; it is only your nose that looks so odd. (*Carolers outside sing "Silent Night"*) Oh, listen, Angelina! Isn't it wonderful! They sing like the angels up in heaven. (*She listens until the voices die away. Then she joins in the singing of the last lines.*) (*Looks at picture on the calendar*) Christmas angel, did you sing when Christ was born? I wish you . . . could talk . . . to . . . me. . . . Christmas Angel. . . . But you are only a . . picture on . . a . . . calendar. (*She begins to hum "Silent night" but gradually falls asleep.*)

(*The door opens and Agatha, Ruth and Dorothy pause on the threshold.*)

Ruth: What a bore to have to walk way over here in the cold! Mother could just as well have sent Bob with the presents.

Agatha: That is what I told her but she made us come.

Dorothy: She said Christmas presents mean more if you give them yourself. Mine looks rather small though — only a pincushion.

Agatha: Mine is a pair of mittens. Mother looked kind of funny when I showed them to her. She thought I should have used more of my allowance, I suppose.

Ruth: Poor people never want the same gifts we do anyway. I'm giving her a book I got last year. There's only a corner torn, and I mended it so that it hardly shows. I couldn't spare any of my allowance; I'm saving it for that big toboggan at Kennedy's.

Agatha: I wonder if I will get the fur coat I asked for — you know, the one with the darling sleeves?

Dorothy: I wonder if I'll get the ring with the square sapphire?

Ruth: Say, maybe no one is at home here. It seems so quiet and dim.

Dorothy: Phoebe must be here. She can't go out unless she is carried. She can't walk a step and you know it!

(*The girls step inside.*)

Agatha: Look! She is asleep in that chair . . . and there's an ugly old doll in her arms.

Dorothy: Let's sneak in quietly and put these packages on the table.

Ruth: I'm glad she's asleep. Now we won't have to stay.

Agatha: I'm eager to get back home and help with the Christmas tree.

Dorothy: It's cold in here and there isn't a sign of anything for Christmas.

Agatha: Come on, let's hurry before she wakes up.

(*An old woman in a long cloak appears at the door.*)

Stranger: Why hurry away when there is so much more to be done here than in your big house, and no hands to do it?

Dorothy: Who are you? We don't know you.

Stranger: No, you don't know me. But I have been listening and I heard your selfish words. Ah, Agatha, your name means "kind and good," and Ruth, yours means "the friend of God." How mistaken they were when they named you!

Ruth: Oh, I don't know Who are you, stranger? You seem to have a great deal to say.

Dorothy: Mother has forbidden us to speak with strangers. Please let us pass.

Stranger: And this is Christmas Eve, when the children who have plenty should especially remember the poor and unfortunate. Have you never thought that He whose birthday you are celebrating was poor? And yet He gave Himself as a gift to us to save us?

Dorothy: (*To Agatha*) I almost wish I had bought that sled for Phoebe, the one with the back.

Agatha: (*To the stranger*) I don't like the way you talk to us, stranger. Poor people don't care for Christmas presents like we do. They are more eager to get something to eat, and our mother will send that. What good would a ring or a muff do Phoebe?

Stranger: How would you know? Have you ever been poor?

Ruth: Of course not. Our father owns the largest factory in the city.

Dorothy: And we kids have a car of our very own to take us to school.

Agatha: Our mother is very fashionable. . . . She has everything she wants. We have a great deal of money.

Stranger: And what does this little one have? (*They look confused.*) She has a brave heart in a painful body and — little else. Her mother works to earn her bread, and has no time to be fashionable.

Agatha: I'm going home. This stranger is very unpleasant. Come on Dorothy. Hurry, Ruth.

(*They exit leaving their packages. The old woman watches them go.*)

Stranger: If I only could send the true meaning of Christmas to these selfish children! (*Her cloak drops from her, and there steps forth an angel all in shining white. She carries a golden shepherd's crook with which she touches Phoebe lightly. Her cloak has disappeared.*)

Phoebe: (*Rubbing her eyes*) What — what are you? Am I dreaming? Surely you look like the Christmas angel on my calendar, but you are really truly alive.

Angel: Do I look like her? (*A group in the background sings "Joy to the World."*)

Angel: I heard you wish for me, so I came to keep you

from being lonesome. What would you like to do to pass the time until your mother comes back?

Phoebe: I don't know. I cannot walk about, you see. I cannot go to the church and I cannot go to Sunday School. I certainly would like to go singing as these other girls do.

Angel: I know. But maybe there is something you could have. The Christchild when He grew up healed many who were completely paralyzed.

Phoebe: You mean, that He could also heal me? And make me like other children? And could I have presents too? But no, that couldn't be. But, who are you stranger?

Angel: I am the Spirit of Christmas. Yes, you may also again be strong and healthy and never lonely if you believe in the Christchild.

Phoebe: Some day shall I really run about to play like other children? Could I even go to Sunday School and have friends?

Angel: That is Christ's gift to you. Look forward to the years before you. Be not afraid, for out of the present shall come great joy. Have faith in Him. To the faithful all things are possible.

Phoebe: Won't you come in for a little while?

Angel: No, I cannot do that; you may only see me from a distance. But each year you will give me a new welcome, and await my coming with happy eyes. A hopeful Christmas, Phoebe. (*Goes out slowly, walking backwards.*)

Phoebe: I have never dreamed of such a lovely one. Oh, Stranger, stay with me. I cannot bear to part with you.

Angel: I must go back to the place from whence your lonely

heart called me. You will not need me any longer, as long as you have Christ in your heart.

Phoebe: How can I thank you for coming to me?

Angel: I do not need your thanks, for I can look deep into your heart and read. I give you the gift of life and purity, and love of him, the child of Bethlehem. A holy Christmas, Phoebe.

Phoebe: Good bye, I wish that you might stay with me.

(Phoebe stretches out her arms. They drop, and she sleeps.)

(Agatha and Dorothy and Ruth appear, dragging a new sled laden with parcels.)

Agatha: *(Softly to someone outside)* Pile the wood near the kitchen door, Bob.

Dorothy: *(Also calling softly)* And put the turkey where Phoebe's mother can find it first thing. Be careful, Ruth; it is very dark in here.

Ruth: I'll say it's dark.

Dorothy: But there's a little glimmer. The candle is just about burning out. Phoebe is still asleep.

Agatha: Let us tiptoe in and fix everything up, all bright and pretty.

(They enter and unwrap some of the packages. One lights two candles, and another arranges a little fir tree on the table.)

Dorothy: I am so glad we had presents that we could give to Phoebe. The stores are all closed, and we couldn't have bought a thing. But that Stranger made me feel so uncomfortable when I thought of the stingy things we were going to give.

Agatha: Me too! Phoebe can ride on this sled if we pull her.

Phoebe: (*Sleepily*) Dear stranger, have you come back again?

Dorothy: It is we, Phoebe. We have come to help you have a merry Christmas.

Agatha: And we brought you some presents.

Phoebe: (*Half awake*) Oh! Thank you. I'm so glad you have come to see me. (*Waking*) Oh! Presents!

Dorothy and Ruth: See! These!

Phoebe: Oh, a doll! And a teddybear!! Just what I wanted.

(*Phoebe hugs the doll and teddy bear*)

Agatha: We'd like to come tomorrow and help you trim the little tree, and we will read the Christmas story to you. May we?

Phoebe: Oh, I'd love to have you. I've wished so very often that you would come in and talk with me.

Agatha: I'm very sorry Phoebe, that we have been so hateful. But if you will let us, we will make up for it. Our mother says she knew your mother years ago; so we should be friends too.

Ruth: I know what would be fun! Tomorrow we will pull you on the sled over to our house and Dorothy and I'll show you our tree and share some of the good things with you.

Phoebe: It seems too good to be true! You are so good to me. I don't like to tell Mumsie. It worries her, but I do get so tired of staying so much alone and never going out.

Agatha: Oh, Phoebe, I am so sorry. Maybe you could come over and see us often if Bob carried you to the car.

Phoebe: I must be dreaming. Pinch me, Agatha. Pinch me hard!

Dorothy: You mustn't look at the rest of these presents until tomorrow. Shall we stay until your mother gets home?

Phoebe: She said she might be late, and it is very dark. Do you think you should?

Ruth: I'll go out and tell Bob to wait for us. He won't mind. The car is warm. (*Exit*)

Dorothy: We have a great big tree. You'll see it tomorrow, and right at the top there is the darlingest angel. (*Carolers begin to sing softly, "It Came upon a Midnight Clear.*)

Phoebe: A Christmas Angel! ! One came to visit me before you came. Maybe I was asleep and dreaming, but she talked to me and a wonderful star was shining on her forehead. (*Re-enter Ruth*)

Ruth: It is all right. We'll stay a while. Oh, listen Agatha .... (*Carolers continue singing, "It Came Upon a Midnight Clear.*")

Phoebe: Oh, I'm so happy. This is the most beautiful Christmas Eve I've ever had. How beautifully they are singing. like angels up in heaven! (*They join in the carol and the carolers sing in full voice as the curtain slowly falls.*)

—A. De Vries
Used with permission of
The Midwest Sunday School Association

13. A BUSINESS MEETING

(A Playlet for Boys)

Cast: Four young men, aged 12-14, representing officers of a Sunday School class.

Scene: Simple business room. Four chairs and a table.

Andy: Well, fellows, let's come to order. What's first on the program?

Bruce: The only thing I know that we have to talk about is what we are going to do with our mission money. You know it is near Christmas, and we ought to send it away so it could be useful at Christmas time.

Andy: O.K. Let's take that first then. How much money have we collected, Bill?

Bill: We have exactly $55 in our mission box.

Bob: Whew! That's quite a lot! How long did it take us to get that much together?

Bill: Well, we started at the beginning of the year and now it's December.

Bruce: Why not send it to the Indian Cousins like we did last year?

Bill : I would rather send it to some special missionary like *Rev. Smith at Shiprock* or *Rev. Randall at Flagstaff* (*Substitute the name of well-known missionaries.*) Often they don't have enough gifts for the children at Christmas. These children certainly need something there.

Bruce: My brother is in the army and he says that the servicemen read everything they can get hold of. How about sending a year's subscription to some Christian magazine to the soldiers?

Bob: Say! That's a good idea! My folks like the *Sunday*

85

School Times and the *Christian Herald.* (*Select magazines known to your group.*)

Andy; Yes! and any of our boys would be glad to see *The Messenger* or *Christian Life* magazine. (*You may wish to select your denominational periodical.*)

Bob: We could use that money to help our radio programs along, too. In that way we can do a lot of Mission work.

Bill: Boy! It's too bad we haven't $55 to give to every one of these causes. It must be nice to be rich and have lots of money to give away.

Bob: Well, maybe some day we'll be rich too. But then, lots of rich people hold on to their money tighter than ever.

Bruce: Well, Christmas is a time when almost everybody feels like giving, so let's hope the rich people will do their bit, too.

Bill: If we could only remember how Jesus gave himself for us, I think we would all be more ready to give to others, too.

Bob: I know I could have given more.

Andy: Yes! You're right! We'd better not criticize the rich people. I guess we could all give more. What do you say about trying to make our Mission fund reach $100 next year?

All: O.K. Let's.

Bob: You know fellows, I just remembered that there are other good causes also right close by. There is *Mr. Cook* who works among the unchurched in our own city. He meets so many poor people. And then there is *Missionary Larson in Chicago.* (*Substitute names of your choice.*)

Andy: Yes, and you know what I was thinking? I was thinking about these thousands of poor war sufferers in

Vietnam and the starving orphans in Korea. I wish we could help them too.

Bruce: I guess it's pretty hard to decide right now about our money. How would it be if we'd talk it over with our families and then decide next Sunday in Sunday School?

Bill: I guess that's best, but I still wish we could remember them all.

Andy: Before we leave boys, I'd like to suggest that we all put a little more pep into our singing in Sunday School. Our superintendent is always complaining that the boys don't sing. Let us show him next Sunday that Mr. _____'s class knows how to do it.

All: O.K. Let's go.

—Midwest Sunday School Association

14. A CHRISTMAS UNIT

This unit was arranged with Primary or Intermediate pupils in mind. The entire class or group is arranged on the platform. The children taking special parts steps forward.

1. SONG: "O Little Town of Bethlehem" (*By the entire group*)

   (*Enter Joseph and Mary; Stand beside cradle.*)

2. FIRST SPEAKER:

   > There they come, foot-sore and weary
   > From far-off Galilee;
   > Faithful Joseph and the Virgin Mary
   > Happy Bethlehem to see.

   > They have come to show obedience
   > To the law of God and man
   > Rich in love and peace and reverence;
   > They the faithful of their clan.

   (*Exit Joseph and Mary*)

3. SONG: "Silent Night" first stanza (*By a quartette, select group, or entire class*)

4. SECOND SPEAKER:

   > Away in a manger,
   > No crib for a bed
   > The little Lord Jesus
   > Laid down His sweet head.

   > The stars in the heaven
   > Looked down where He lay
   > The little Lord Jesus
   > Asleep in the hay.

> The cattle are lowing
> The baby awakes
> But little Lord Jesus
> No crying He makes.
>
> I love Thee, Lord Jesus!
> Look down from the sky,
> And stay by my cradle
> Till morning is nigh.

5. SONG: "Joy to the World" (*By the entire class*)

(*Enter Shepherds*)

6. THIRD SPEAKER:

> Shepherds true their watch are keeping
> In the fields of Bethlehem;
> While the city lies asleeping
> A heavenly angel comes to them.
>
> "Fear not," speaks the angel gladly,
> "Tidings of great joy I bring;
> Christ is born in David's city,
> In a manger you will find Him."
>
> Then a multitude of angels
> Sings a heavenly song to them;
> "Glory in the highest heavens
> Peace on earth, good will to men."

7. SONG: "While Shepherds Watched Their Flocks by Night" (*The class*)

(*Exit Shepherds*)

8. FOURTH SPEAKER:

> Why do bells of Christmas ring?
> Why do little children sing?

Once a lovely shining star
Seen by shepherds from afar
Gently moved until the light
Made a manger cradle bright.
There a darling baby lay
Pillowed soft upon the hay.
And His mother sang and smiled,
"This is Christ, the Holy Child."

So the bells of Christmas ring
So the little children sing.

9. SINGING: (*Entire class*)

Boys: Who came down from heaven to earth?
Girls: Jesus Christ, our Savior.
Boys: Came a child of lowly birth?
Girls: Jesus Christ, our Savior.
All: Sound the chorus loud and clear,
He has brought salvation near,
None so precious, none so dear,
Jesus Christ, our Savior.

10. SONG: "Christmas Comes to One and All" (Tune: "Jesus Loves Me") (*Entire class*)

Christmas comes to one and all,
Christmas comes to great and small,
Christ was born in Bethlehem
Left His heavenly home for men.

Chorus:

Christ loves the children
Christ loves the children,
Christ loves the children,
The children of the world.

Jesus loves the black and white,
Yellow, red, and brown alike;
Came to earth all those to save
Freely them His blessing gave.

—Josephine Baker

(After brief pause, the children sing with bowed heads)

Into my heart, into my heart,
Come into my heart, Lord Jesus,
Come in today, come in to stay,
Come into my heart, Lord Jesus.

—Arranged by M. Arnoys
Used with permission of
The Midwest Sunday School Association